How To Live With A

PAMPERED PET

ERIC GURNEY

With Text by William Nettleton

PRENTICE-HALL, Inc., Englewood Cliffs, New Jersey

Library of Congress Catalog Card Number: 65-23065

Printed in the United States of America

T 41559

PRENTICE-HALL INTERNATIONAL, INC., *London*
PRENTICE-HALL OF AUSTRALIA, PTY., LTD., *Sydney*
PRENTICE-HALL OF CANADA, LTD., *Toronto*
PRENTICE-HALL OF INDIA (PRIVATE) LTD., *New Delhi*
PRENTICE-HALL OF JAPAN, INC., *Tokyo*

To my Mother and Dad

CONTENTS

1 Pet History

Getting washed for dinner.

A lion that looked as if it had more teeth than a crocodile came up to the two sleeping figures and licked one of them on the face. The recipient of this attention woke up, stretched, then asked the lion to depart because its tongue was a little rough. The lion, being a perfect gentlelion, bowed politely and left. In this manner Adam and Eve were awakened in Eden. They had breakfast, and as there was no job for Adam to go to and no dishes for Eve to wash, they searched around for something to pass the time. They decided to give each animal a name. As we can see, man had pets before he even had clothes.

Adam and Eve went out into the garden and began to name animals. They started off with simple names such as lion, cat, dog,

The first whirl around the maypole.

cow, lamb. However, with time the names became more eloquent, if not more beautiful. Thus we have "aardvark" which can put a kink in the tongue, and "duckbilled platypus" which will take it out again.

One day, while Adam was swinging with some simian friends, Eve was out looking at the apple tree which bore the one fruit they were forbidden to eat. That's when she met the cutest animal of all, a talking snake. He could not only say "aardvark" and "duckbilled platypus" with ease, but he had no difficulty with "Peter Piper picked a peck of pickled peppers." This should have made Eve suspicious. The snake had a great deal to say about apples, and later in the day Eve batted her eyes at Adam a couple of times and persuaded him to pick one. They split it, and ate it. It was probably bitter, wormy, and still green, resembling the knowledge it was supposed to impart. They learned then that not all animals are pets. They also got kicked out of Eden.

An apple a day keeps the doctor away.

A good breakfast is the most important meal of the day.

Things were quite different on the outside. The Lord had painted everything with a big brush. There were dinosaurs. These creatures were so stupid that if you kicked them in the tail, they wouldn't feel it until next Thursday. It should not be construed that this collection of oddities didn't love Adam and Eve. On the contrary, they loved them to pieces and that was exactly how they

intended to leave them. Adam tried giving orders to a *tyran-nosaurus rex*, but he was not sure whether the message had reached its brain, or whether it had a brain to reach in the first place. Therefore Adam and Eve retreated, with all dignity possible, to the nearest cave. At this time, it might truly be said, animals kept men in cages.

The first pet man had was probably brought home by the children after they had found it hurt. Father was all for popping it in the frying pan, except that it wouldn't fit and it whistle-growled menacingly. So Father allowed the children to keep it. We don't know the name of the first pet or what it ate. Perhaps it was called "the thing." This creature was so grateful for man's kindness that it brought back something edible to the cave. This gave man an idea. If he had to earn his bread by the sweat of his brow, he would make the animals help him. This is called poetic justice, and it usually works out only in poetry.

The children loved it dearly. It lived 932 years, which is quite surprising considering it ate nothing but boiled bolyglops.

Man promptly looked around to see what other animals were suitable. Many experiments ended in disaster until he came across the cat and dog and noticed that they were small. This gave man a good chance of surviving the training period. Eventually he found animals that would not only hunt for him, but would also carry him from place to place—like the horse. The elephant and the camel were less common, and eventually the horse became the real status thing. You were hardly anybody at all without a neolithic nag.

With all kinds of animals working for him, the world began to look pretty good to early man, but actually by the time Noah arrived on the scene, things were in pretty sad shape. The Lord decided He was going to do something about it. He told Noah to build an ark. The Ark was about as compact as the Queen Mary, and its construction took most of Noah's spare time for about a hundred years. When it was finished, Noah sat back to have a mug of mead and a nip of nectar while he admired his handiwork.

About this time the Lord reminded Noah that he was going to have to round up two of every creature in the world. This made Noah spill his drink. What, two? Of everything? Noah mumbled a couple of times under his breath and started on his chore. If rounding up lions seems difficult, imagine the problems involved with insects! Noah had to corral a male and female of every species before the magnifying glass had even been invented!

Rounding up . . . . .

wild animals . . . . .

is a sport which . . . . .

should be left . . . . . .

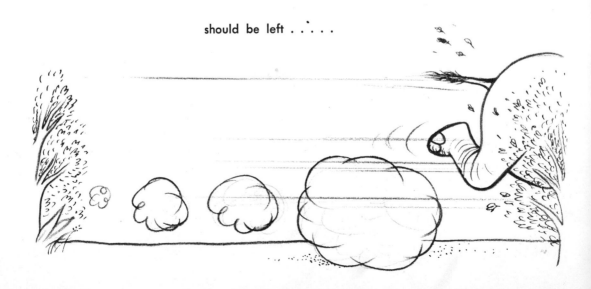

in the hands . . . . .

of an expert.

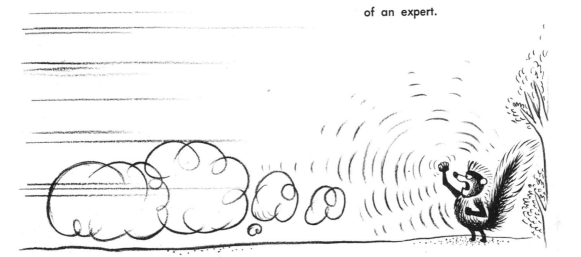

It was easy to lead the lions aboard.

You mean you don't remember where you found it?

Finally the rains arrived and the Ark became the largest floating zoo in the world. A long time passed before the dove brought back the olive branch and the Lord spread His rainbow in the sky. Then Noah did two things which few captains have ever done. He deliberately ran his ship aground; then he abandoned the hulk ahead of everyone else. Why not?

The first land rush.

I may be puny, but I'm potent,

It must have been a long time before man had any pets after that. But eventually he was at it again. And most of the pets we know today have come into existence since the flood. Once again the horse became the super-status pet, and on Long Island, still is. Many people have been known to fall under the spell of this quadruped. Alexander the Great had Bucephalus, and General Lee had Traveler.

Say, "Cheese."

It said, "Get up on the right side."

But then, just as now, there were "in" pets and "out" pets. Ocelots today, weasels tomorrow. Cleopatra had panthers and at least one unfriendly asp. European monarchs favored falcons and the potentates of the East elected elephants. The Caesars preferred peacocks for their finery while Roman lions found Christians crunchy.

Love can be a growing pain.

Two squeaks and a croak.

All these pets were good for something. Falcons could catch rabbits; elephants could carry maharajas; peacocks could be eaten. The asp had a function to perform for Cleopatra, and panthers provided an adequate solution for discarded lovers. But today we have pets that are absolutely useless: Dogs that wouldn't know a rabbit from an old shoe, cats that abhor mice, and birds that do nothing all the day long but sharpen their beaks on cuttlefish bones and admire themselves in the mirror. Not only that, now we are engaged in phase three of the operation by bringing creatures home that are not only useless but out-and-out dangerous.

2 Children—The Original Pet Lovers

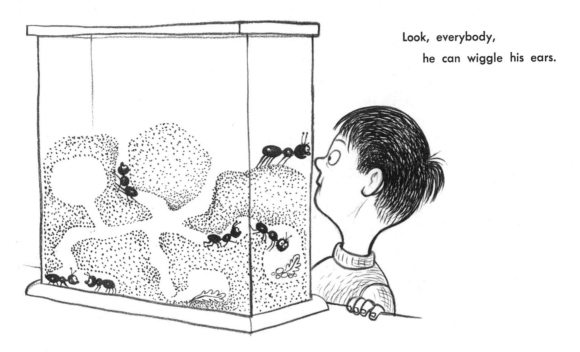

Look, everybody,
he can wiggle his ears.

It all began, as we suggested, with "the thing" that the children brought home to the cave. Children have a knack for making friends with animals, and most of the pets we have today are the result of children's encounters with animals in the woods, swamps, and ponds. The kinds of pets children bring home are still the most common, along with cats and dogs.

The animals plan it this way. Rapport is the answer. Rapport is something that happens when a child looks into the beady little eyes of a frog, a mouse, a sick crow, a snake, or a turtle, and the creature looks back soulfully. Probably the reason so many of these creatures let themselves be captured is the promise of a nice home where they will be fed; it is a bothersome chore to hunt up your own food or to worry about heat, light, and water.

Intelligent animals let themselves be caught only by children. They know a child will not be too discriminating about what he brings back. The thought of providing the animal with a cage never enters a child's head until he arrives home. The youngster will be able to feed his pet almost anything, and the pet will miraculously survive. Let an adult feed, say, a bullfrog, anything but flies, and the old croaker will croak in more ways than one. But little Johnny can feed it bacon or the leftover oatmeal which he can't stand. He can carry it around in his pocket all day long to frighten the teacher at school, and make it perform all kinds of unbullfroglike acts, and the bullfrog will thrive.

There can be only one large frog in a small pond.

The lack of a cage is no problem. Bullfrogs have been kept in almost anything but small wine bottles. Turtles, too, need no special attention—they bring their cage with them. In addition some have the distinct advantage of being able to bite. Junior can carry around large snapping turtles and get away with it. Adults hardly dare look cross-eyed at one.

When one loses something of value . . . . .

the inclination is to rush . . . . .

out haphazardly in a slipshod . . . . .

fashion . . . . .

to obtain a suitable . . . . .

replacement.

I knew a shortcut through the bed wouldn't work out.

These first-found pets are part of a larger plan. They are the forerunners of the invasion to come—the commandoes, the first wave. The plan of attack is simple. Phase One is for the frogs and the turtles to create as much consternation as possible among the adults in the household. The adults, then, promise to get the child a more conventional caged pet such as a parakeet or hamster, or a dog or cat. In come the prolific hamsters, the white mice, the cats, the dogs, the ant farms, and Phase Two is under way.

Warm martini, anybody?

The animals conducting Phase Two are usually capable of establishing rapport with the whole family. They win everyone over by performing some useful service or by looking woebegone. They get into trouble every once in a while just to let you know they are around.

Before investing and losing . . . . .

money in watered stock . . . . .

it is a good idea . . . . .

to hire a good financial advisor . . . . .

and give him free rein . . . . .

to insure . . . . .

yourself of adequate returns.

Sometimes when a new pet . . . . .

arrives in a new home . . . . .

rather extensive . . . . .

renovations and adjustments . . . . .

by family members . . . . .

must be made . . . . .

to insure . . . . .

the well-being of . . . . .

all concerned.

When Junior grows up he will not remember when the ants got out of the ant farm and the small holes began to appear in the woodwork, or the time the hamster took a tour of the family plumbing which cost about as much as flying first-class across the Atlantic. Forgotten are the scratches suffered when the dog trotted off with the roast beef, the flurry of excitement when Father almost lynched himself while scaling a tree for the cat that wouldn't come down. Yes, the secret of being happy is certainly being healthy and having a short memory.

3 Fish at Home and Abroad

Jonah was the first human ever to make friends with a member of the aquatic kind. During a storm Jonah, who had been on deck drinking to drown his sorrows, got washed overboard with a cask of brandy, and nearly drowned himself instead. As the ship disappeared over the horizon, Jonah was just about to go down for the third time. Fortunately, however, this creature swam alongside. When Jonah saw it, he didn't believe it any more than he believed the little pink elephants with which he was also having trouble. This creature had a green eye to starboard and a red eye to port. Of course it was made up especially for the occasion and spoke excellent Hebrew. The creature asked Jonah who he was and how he was enjoying his swim. After Jonah had told his tale the creature cried, because what he liked best were nice fat juicy packet passengers. He had tried a couple of prophets earlier, but they were so tough and stringy that they had given him horrible indigestion for a couple of months and finally he had to spit them up, still alive and kicking, on a tropical island. So the creature started to swim away. But he was a kindly creature. Even when he ate packet passengers, he ate them gently, and it made him sick at hearts, all seven of them, to be leaving Jonah to drown in a wine-dark sea. So he offered Jonah a ride inside. At first Jonah declined. However, the creature told Jonah about the ship's library and about a stove he had swallowed over which Jonah could toast his toes. So Jonah, unable to argue any more, let himself be swallowed by a whale.

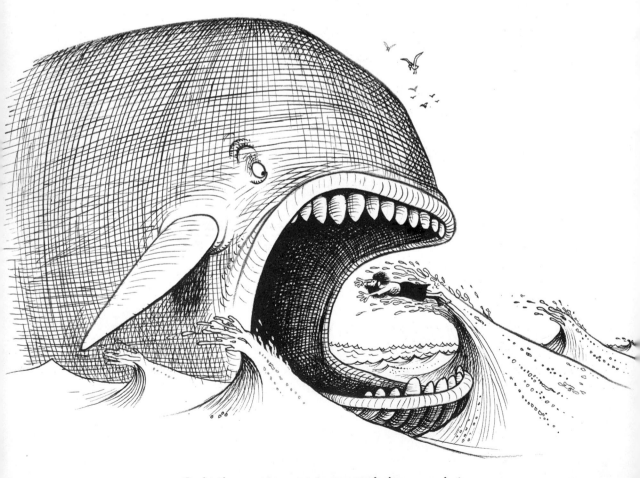

Cocktail canapés come in assorted shapes and sizes.

Guppies are the most common fish kept at home. But anyone can raise guppies, and big guppies are quite content to eat little guppies, so something rarer is continually being sought—like the archer fish. In the tropics this interesting little fellow squirts a drop of water at some insect. At home he can put out the end of a cigarette at twenty feet. For even more excitement there is the

Yesterday it got three light bulbs and a parakeet.

lion-fish, *Pterois Volitans*, whose sting will make your hair stand on end, or the piranha whose teeth are sharp enough to cut your hair off. Both of these fish make wonderful prestige pets and excellent conversation pieces. People will "ooh" and "ah" if you have been stung by one or bitten by the other. Of course they will "ooh" and "ah" without any prompting from you if they are bitten or stung themselves.

Today it's smiling because
it bit somebody.

The one with gravy spots had a better flavor.

Electric eels are also charming. They must be handled with rubber gloves for reasons too obvious to mention. However, there was the case of the advanced aquarist whose young son cut a patch out of one of the rubber gloves in an attempt to repair a defunct balloon. When Father reached in with his rubber gloves to hook the electric eel to the lights on the Christmas tree, he got lit instead. It caged his eyeballs for a week.

The last man who tried this is now an ash.

Generally . . . . .

meals are served . . . . .

on all first-class flights.

For years it seemed the closest man was ever going to get to the fish was by having aquariums. Now, with the recent development of scuba equipment man is able to go right into the ocean where most of the fish live. However, even after sending down an ambassadress, Claire Boothe Luce—and she should certainly know how to make friends—no success can be reported in man's attempt to make friends with the fish. Every type of individual has tried—stunt men, charming television personalities, and lovely starlets—all without success. Men have even played music to fish and fed them underwater hors d'oeuvres, and all we have learned is that though people will eat fish sometimes, fish are glad to eat people all the time, and any day of the week will do.

You should see the one that got away.

An example of brilliant deduction.

There is an exception: The porpoise, fishlike but not a fish, is an enemy of sharks and a friend of man. Porpoises, who have a perpetual smile, have been known to push drowning seamen to shore. But just as often they have nudged them out to sea. The only trouble with porpoises is their intellect. They may be smarter than we are. Attempts are being made to teach them to talk. We all hope they will say, "Hello, friend," but secretly we suspect they may say, "Today the ocean, tomorrow the world." This would put a severe strain on shore-to-sea diplomatic relations.

Keeping porpoises is, of course, difficult and expensive unless you can make them do tricks and charge admission. The expense starts off with the salt water; you must have a few million gallons of it properly aerated, properly saline, and with the proper minerals in it. For their food the Fulton Fish Market is probably adequate. Porpoises are the super-prestige pet of the aquatic kind. Of course they will probably be superseded by whales and eventually by the most feared creature of all, the man-eating shark. Perhaps in the future we will have such a shark, named Aloysius and properly trained to eat nothing but spinach. We hope not. However, it is safe to say they won't become house pets, isn't it?

4 How to Avoid Snakes and Other Reptiles

Taking on a load of anti-venom.

Dead Eye Pete was staggering through Rattlesnake Gulch after having had a couple of bottles of firewater at the Last Chance Saloon. Dead Eye was a prospector of the old school, a man who could hold his liquor and smell gold sixty miles away but never find any. So there he was out in the gulch with his old mule, Bessie. Why he wanted to prospect in Rattlesnake Gulch must remain a mystery. He hadn't gone very far before he was bitten one or two times by a large and angry rattlesnake. This sobered Pete up considerably, but the snake died.

Man has been hesitant about making friends with snakes ever since his sad experience with the talking one in Eden. However, there are people who keep snakes as pets. Take the Indian fakir with his basketful of cuddly cobra. The fakir is supposed to lure the snake out of the basket by tootling on a flute. But snakes can't hear. Once the snake has got his dander up, he is supposed to weave back and forth to the beat of the music. Actually he is watching the flute. Now a dash of cobra venom is more than mud in your eye—yet most fakirs don't wear eye patches. The reason for this is that most of the cobras have been disarmed—which is one of the things that makes fakirs fakirs in the first place.

A . . . . .

mongoose in the hand . . . . .

is worth two cobras in the bush.

And there's enough left for a couple of half hitches.

Though you may not win friends, you will certainly influence people with a pet snake. When troubled by late-staying guests, simply wrap nine or ten feet of boa constrictor, king snake, or rock python around your neck and walk into the midst of the party, if you are still able to breathe. Your living room will soon look like a disaster area, but the guests will have left. This peculiar response evoked by snakes has further uses. You can leave your home for as long as a month with a couple of snakes roaming around and have fair surety that no burglars will bother anything.

The greens are easy enough; it's the reds that hurt.

Though snakes have their advantages, there are other reptiles worth mentioning here, though not necessarily worth having. There is the iguana, a lizard that looks like a bad dream. He bites. There is the chameleon, but chameleons eat mealworms and mealworms don't grow on trees. Perhaps the most popular of the reptiles is the alligator.

I took the wrong drain somewhere.

The only trouble with the alligators is they grow up. There is a rumor—unfortunately it is not true—that large hunting expeditions are conducted in the sewer systems of New York City to get rid of the monstrous alligators which were, at one time, pets. It has even been suggested that the reason so many of the streets of New York are torn up is to repair the damage caused by ricocheting bullets that have punctured telephone cables, water pipes, and gas lines. To keep the streets of New York in good repair, it is suggested that an ordinance be passed at once to prevent alligators from growing larger than billfold size. Frankly, our preference for alligators is in the form of handbags.

It should not be assumed from what has been said that we are not fond of snakes and other reptiles. We might even make quite a case for them. For instance, they do not need to be fed very often. Any snake, unless he is a compulsive eater, is content to have one meal a month. You do not have to amuse these pets, and if you let them out of their cage you can make a dull life more interesting—if not shorter. However, as far as we are concerned, snakes can stay where they are, and we will move just a little bit over this way.

5 Birds and Birdbrains

Perched on the pinnacle of success.

Baron Gustave A. Diddlebock awakened. He propped himself up on six pillows and gave the bell cord a solid yank, summoning to his presence a butler, a hairdresser, his breakfast, a basin of scented water, and other necessary luxuries escorted by various footmen. An hour later, looking every inch a Diddlebock, Gustave emerged triumphantly from his boudoir in the latest hunting fashion. There was a faint sneer on his face as he strode down the corridor past the portraits of all the Diddlebocks who had gone before. He stopped a long time in front of the portrait of Humphrey the Great. Though the Diddlebocks all had been falconers, Humphrey had been the greatest. He had traded his one-hundred-and-ninety room castle for an English falcon named Spitfire.

Gustave had decided to outfalcon Humphrey. He had purchased a new secret weapon which stood three inches taller than its master, a large and vicious Argentinian condor. The Diddlebock condor was named Gertrude after Gustave's mother-in-law, and it had all that worthy lady's foul disposition. When the condor was launched on its first test flight, in pursuit of a rabbit, things began to come apart. The first launching was a ricochet off a turtle;

Hard-shelled rabbits are a traumatic experience to any hunting bird.

the second knocked Gustave off into a patch of thorns, while the huge shadow of the bird frightened the rabbit into its hole. Thwarted, the great condor veered and chased the Diddlebock's prize bull, Lumpknuckle III, into the river where it was run over by a ferry boat and drowned. At that moment the art of falconry as a sport took a downhill turn.

Oops.

Trained birds haven't done much for mankind since then, and most birds still remain outside the home. Those we have taken inside, confined to cages, may be divided roughly into three classes. There are those that sing, those that talk, and happily, those that do nothing at all. The singing birds used to be the most popular. Of these the canary held first place for a long time.

William Tell was famous for this, only he used an arrow.

Wood is where you find it.

Who killed Cock Robin?

However, the canary's popularity has been on the wane, over-
taken by those birds that talk—the parrot, the mynah, and the
parakeet. Talking birds, in our opinion, are hardly an advantage. First, they don't know what they are talking about. Second,
it takes a long time to teach them to talk. The most common
method is by playing a record over and over again until they learn

a few pithy phrases. The recording may amuse you for the first few minutes; after that you will want to put on earmuffs to deaden the repetition. If you can't stand the record that is supposed to teach the bird, what will you do when the bird starts to talk? The phonograph can be turned off, the bird is equipped with no such button.

Taking a whirl at a language.

Parrots are the best of the talking birds. They live so very long that they can be handed down like the family silver, from generation to generation. However, parrots are slow in learning to speak.

The first intelligent word in ninety-five years.

Oh, for a stainless steel razor.

One runs the risk of having a silent parrot for ninety-five years, and then a constant stream of invective for the next ten. The parakeet lives a much shorter time and is smaller than the parrot, with the result that it can't bite as often or as badly. It is one of the few birds allowed outside of a cage to mingle with the family. Parakeets have been known to learn many tricks like pulling cigarettes out of a pack—or taking a bath in a martini which doesn't add to the flavor or the feathers. Of course, our preference is for birds that do absolutely nothing but sit on a perch all day long,

They both eat sunflower seeds.

and eat seeds. Such birds, unlike parrots, cause no worries when ministers or maiden aunts come to visit. Nor do we have to wonder what all the whistling is about. We know that it is the kettle, or something wrong somewhere. Finches are ideal birds to have. They don't make a sound. They sit on a perch contemplating each other in mutual admiration. And you don't have to worry about them trying to get into the swim of things during your next cocktail party either.

Birds need a minimum amount of care. All that is needed is a cage, a perch, a watering trough, a feeder, feed, gravel, paper for the bottom of the cage, some molting medicine to help him shed his feathers, some wheat germ oil to keep his feathers in pristine condition, a beak trimmer to keep him from biting (the use of which leads precisely to the results it was designed to prevent), a stand to keep the cage off the floor and out of drafts, some mite medicine for those times when mites bother him, a

They're wearing it short this year.

mirror so that he can look at himself and keep from growing lonely, a cuttlefish bone on which to sharpen his beak so that he can peck his food properly and peck you whenever you get too close. If you want to teach him how to talk or sing, there are the additional requirements of phonograph and records, and a pair of earmuffs for yourself. We have actually known a couple who managed to cram all this paraphernalia into a single automobile though it took some doing.

6 Insects, Why?

After a hard day's work it's good to get home for dinner.

There was once a flea circus owner—a venerable impresario—Mortimer P. Smoskapopski. He was one of the great flea trainers of all time, and we hope that history will reserve a small line for him some day. During his era he trained fleas to pull miniature wagons and miniature cannons. He had flea tumbling acts, and he had actually managed to train his star performer, a beauteous flea aerialist who bit to the name Mabel, to walk the high wire which was a piece of dental floss suspended between two toothpicks. During one evening performance, a dog managed to get inside the circus. Mabel, who had become rather tired of living in a match box, took off with the entire troupe.

Thank God! They aren't termites.

After this tragic loss, Mr. Smoskapopski, determined to let by-gones be bygones, recovered admirably and became a vice-president of an insecticide company. His specialty was flea powder for dogs.

Probably the only insects sensible to have as pets are the ones stuck on pins under glass, with neatly typewritten labels for the sake of those who really want to know. However, we must admit that ant farms are owned by quite reasonable, even extremely intelligent people. It is, nevertheless, a good idea to know something about ants before investing in an ant farm, because there are ants and ants, and not just any ant will do. Take the case of the Ash family whose son George managed to acquire an almost vacated ant farm from the boy next door for a broken ball-point pen and a jar of lightning bugs. George got some ants, all right.

I don't mind riding bareback as long as he doesn't jump.

One day he left the cork out of the top of the cage. He returned just in time to see the last one fly away. George's father shortly became an expert on termites and wore a harried look for years.

Often a genuine antique can be determined by the presence of small wormholes.

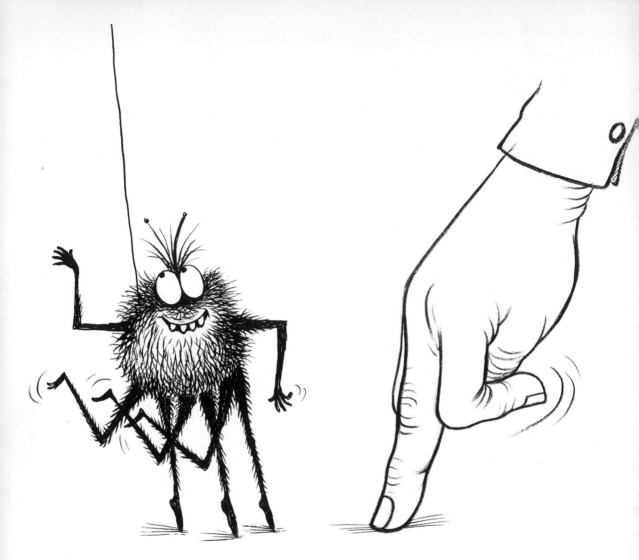

Dance on its toes and it will bite you.

Perhaps the most unusual of the insects which people have been known to keep as pets is the tarantula. We cannot imagine how anyone except a dancer could find a sense of rapport with such a big, hairy, venomous creature. Tarantulas, during their mating season, perform a courtship dance which looks a little like the "twist." It has even been suggested that that dance was inspired by the tarantula. If that is true, it was probably inspired

They haven't had a salesman in seventeen years.

by a tarantula dropping down the back of a low-cut gown at a society ball. Frankly, we don't like tarantulas, and we don't like other insects. We don't particularly dislike them either, except when they bite. They can stay in their area of the world, and we will stay in ours, though it is too bad they can't all be shipped to the North Pole and pickled in a glacier.

7 Mammalian Madness

Chipped Chippendale on toast, the gourmet's delight.

The creatures in the previous chapters are good for absolutely nothing but to frighten people, make noise, or bite. But they are kept in cages. Most mammals are not. Most mammals are allowed the run of the household. In other words, the house becomes their cage. The rodents such as the guinea pig, the rabbit, the hamster, the mouse, and other creatures too horrible to mention here are the mammals that are kept in cages. Rodents continually have to sharpen their teeth, and if allowed loose are just as likely to try a piece of Chippendale as a piece of firewood. This lack of discrimination on their part and the prolific intensity with which they bear offspring are reasons enough to lock them up. It has been said of rabbits that in the course of six years two rabbits could produce nearly six million other rabbits without any help from Dr. Spock.

One good turn . . . . .

deserves another.

Anchovy layer cakes are a lost art.

Of course our contention is that no animal should be allowed loose in the house, though we do not follow our own preaching. The most common house-mammal is the cat. There are thirty million cats, more or less, in this country alone. In addition, there are about twenty million dogs. These two kinds of pets have provided indispensable services to mankind. In Egypt the cat's

AQUARIUM

Every once in a while it is fun to dine out.

ability to get rid of rodents made him a god. However, here there are about twenty-nine million, nine hundred and ninety-nine thousand cats that have a well-developed phobia against rats and mice. They wouldn't know what a mouse was unless it was made of wool stuffed with catnip.

Build a better rattrap and the world won't beat a path to your door.

Dogs have also provided services of note to mankind. The dog is a natural protector and protects his master against mailmen, milkmen, garbage collectors, delivery boys, and guests. However, it seems that all burglars today are dog-proof. Burglars never seem to be bitten by dogs at all. Not only is the dog a protector, as we have just seen; there is a myth still perpetuated by some sporting magazines that dogs actually have been known to help man hunt, that they can find game and point out birds and chase foxes. Of course, we don't believe such foolishness. We have seen

But mine, dear, has two dials.

thousands and thousands of dogs and most of them don't even know where they buried the bone in the backyard. As for chasing down game . . . well, we have observed them chasing tennis balls, golf balls, airplanes, automobiles, sticks, and a host of very respectable people.

There are only three calories in herringbone twill.

In addition to the cat and dog we should make a proud entry of that champion of all champions of prestige symbols: the horse, of course. The horse used to take knights to the battlefield, drag plows, carry messages, and transport people across town or across the world. A number of wealthy people own horses. But the modern horse is different from the old-fashioned variety. Often enough the modern horse goes where it wants to go; less often it goes where the rider wants. However, riding is good exercise, and if the path through the brambles seems rough at times, one can only be thankful that the horse didn't go into the swamp. It is also good exercise to walk twenty-three miles back to the stable after being dumped unceremoniously into a puddle. Of course, the horse requires shoeing, currying, feeding, clipping, saddling, bridling, watering, breaking, and training. These are good exercises too. Some are dangerous.

One billion and a half dollars, give or take a few million, are spent per annum on the cats and dogs of this country alone. They form a solid cornerstone in our financial system, so we have to be in favor of them. Besides we have six or seven ourselves. And because we also like horses, especially when they win, we are in favor of them, too. But the rest are madness.

It took hours to get the right shade of black.

And now for a rousing chorus of *On Moonlight Bay*.

There's no substitute for a good hot-water bottle.

The seal, the bear, the lion, the chimpanzee, the de-scented skunk, the otter, the kinkajou, the coatimundi, and others of this kind rightfully belong either in a zoo or in a circus, or out in the woods, or behind barbed wire, or securely fastened in steel cages,

Someone won't get the point.

or simply in museums—stuffed—which is the way we like them the best. The idea of having these animals in the house must have come from the circus. In circuses they manage to do incredible feats: Monkeys and bears ride bicycles; seals balance balls on their noses or tootle on flutes; lions jump through hoops of fire. But they don't entertain in the home. The audience is too small.

It takes at least thirty feet to stop after applying the brakes.

All he had to say was "Please."

As an example of what can happen with such creatures in the house, take the case of the Tuttletons who owned a de-scented skunk, named Myrtle.

The Tuttletons were having a cocktail party at their country home. It was spring, and the doors were open to the patio, to the front yard, to the back yard. Myrtle, of course, was the center of attention. Everybody picked her up and patted her and pushed so many cocktail canapés down her gullet that she began to feel like a broken vending machine. She was picked up and petted so much that she traveled about fourteen miles without ever touching the floor. Finally she managed to escape and stagger outside.

After six martinis, a Mr. Filch saw one skunk coming in through the front door, one coming in through the back door, and one coming in from the patio. Thinking his martini might be the cause of his triple vision, Mr. Filch dumped the remains into a large pot containing the Tuttleton's prize rubber tree which promptly expired. He replenished the glass with straight gin and exhaled the appropriate amount of vermouth across the top. Then he saw three skunks because there were three skunks. Of course, only one was Myrtle. When it was all over, Myrtle surveyed the disastrous wake of the departing guests and smiled.

Who invited the country cousins?

If a simple animal like a de-scented skunk can cause such consternation, what about other animals, which are generally quicker on their feet and often more intelligent? Take the otter.

To remove otter tracks use a good grade of bleach.

Otters are very fond of playing in the water. Suppose after a couple of months of home adjustment the otter learned how to turn the water on, but not how to turn it off? How about those animals with claws that scratch, like the ordinary house cat? If house cats are hard on chairs what could bigger cats do to a grand piano? Probably play it like a harp.

And the janitor can't swim.

The worst kinds of pets among the animals are the three-dimensional pets, those that are not content merely to walk on the floor on all fours, but must walk about on two feet and climb things. Among these are the monkey, the kinkajou, the coatimundi.

What do you mean I can't bring it back?

They can open drawers, and do; they have picked locks, turned on electric appliances, set off burglar alarms, and loosed the local constabulary on endless hunts. With the modernization of the telephone system so that it is now impossible to dial anything without getting something and being charged for it, having a monkey can be a financial catastrophe. Although, the cost of having one of these pets probably wouldn't be affected appreciably by a dozen calls to Hong Kong in one month.

As always, the senior partner collects all the money while the junior partner does all the work.

These pets do not mean to be destructive. They are just mimicking you. You turn on the thermostat. They turn it up to a hundred and three because they can't read. You turn on the gas and light it. They turn on the gas and look around for the match box, puzzle over how to get it open, twenty minutes later finally manage, and then try to light it. Hopefully they won't succeed.

Frankly, the three-dimensional pets frighten us. The only one we would recommend is a monkey that we saw the other day in a

I would invite you in, but the house is a mess.

toy shop. It runs on batteries. As for the rest of the mammals, they aren't too bad as long as they aren't too big. We suggest, if you are going to have a mammal as a pet, that you be satisfied with one small and easily frightened dog or a cat. However, if you wish to find out about having another kind, give one to a friend first. See if he is still talking to you at the end of the month, and make sure to inspect his home frequently. Observe your friend for any new twitches or unnatural mannerisms. Or better yet, don't give the pet to a friend. Give it to an enemy.

8 Pet Influences

The plucked after the plucker.

Barney Bildad Belcher sat under a tree, a piece of straw sticking out of the corner of his mouth. He was hard at work thinking. At least that was what he told his wife. Actually he was watching the birds fly, and he was watching the bees fly, and he was watching the butterflies, bats, moths, and hummingbirds fly. And with all this flying going on, he came to the conclusion that he himself might be able to fly. So he got some feathers, and a couple of pieces of wood and he made himself some wings which he strapped on with a couple of old belts. He took off like a bolt of lightning, after a rather short and harried run from a cliff that overlooked his neighbor's greenhouse. The bill for the broken glass persuaded Barney to experiment no further and to look upon all birds with

A spider does it to catch flies, a man because it is there.

If it's an English mole, you pass on the right.

some degree of suspicion. Barney's mistake was in watching the wrong birds. The Wright brothers at Kittyhawk had watched hawks, the right kind of bird for their purposes. Barney should have watched an owl and stuck to thinking.

Man has received far-reaching gifts from the animals. A good many of man's inventions were invented by animals first. The spider invented pulleys. Other animals, perhaps the elephant, may have given us the idea of building cranes. The mole may have suggested there was something worthwhile underground.

I live in a zoo.   I work in one.

Animals have invaded our language to an alarming degree: "He's as grouchy as a bear," "tenacious as a bulldog," "as charming as a viper," and the like. The Indians went so far as to name themselves after animals. There was Chief Sitting Bull who didn't do an awful lot of sitting, much to General Custer's consternation; Running Fawn who, as far as her husband was concerned, didn't run far enough, and Crazy Horse who was, of course, not crazy at all.

(Sly fox.)

(Don't be a pig.)
Corn oil is full of polyunsaturated fats.

(That silly ass.)
I don't know what I ate, but it tickled all the way down.

(Queer birds.)
A flock of robins returning from Disneyland.

Another weather prediction comes to naught.

Chief Sitting Bull in a war council with a top aide.

Chief Crazy Horse and his dancing
partner at a hoedown.

We have so many animals in our language it is almost impossible to speak English without mentioning them. We have poodle cuts, the Yale bulldog, the Russian bear, the English lion, the Navy goat and the Army jackass. We have mink coats, ermine wraps, sable blankets, chinchilla earmuffs, sheepskin linings, kidskin gloves, and alligator handbags. And as if this weren't enough, we have the Beatles (sic).

Three cheers for me, enormous friend,
I pulled a thorn so your foot would mend;
And because you are a generous fellow,
I know you'll reward me with a bellow.
But please, I beg you, don't get mad—
As a doormat, I would be very sad.

Most of these influences have done us little harm. But an acquaintance of ours, whose hobby is being a professional alarmist, disturbed us one evening with a new project of his. He suggested that a league be formed called the Anti-Pet and Anti-Animal League for the Preservation of People (APAALPP).

He argued that man has come to have some skill in handling animals. Those animals that at one time used to hunt us or be hunted by us are now invited into the house without the slightest qualm. The next step is obvious. People don't eat cats and dogs because they are pets. If the other animals become pets we won't be able to eat meat, and as soon as we learn how to make friends with the fish, we won't be able to eat them either. This will make us all vegetarians.

Already, our acquaintance pointed out, the population explosion among pets is threatening to overwhelm our own. More pet stores are opening than ever before. There are more veterinarians coming of age than MDs, and more hospitals are being built for pets than for humans. Of course we shook our heads over this state of affairs and were about to sign on the dotted line and join APAALPP. But when we were asked to get rid of our three dogs, five cats, two turtles, and one parrot, we quickly withdrew.

It's not whether you win or lose but how you play the game.

Ever since, we have looked very studiously at the animals who run our households pretty much as they will. We are beginning to realize there is some truth to his words. The pets are taking over everything. They interfere with our travels because someone has to feed them when we are gone. They do pretty much as they please and pretend to be stone deaf when we want them to do something. They have taken over our living room and requisitioned all the best chairs. Obviously they are enjoying all the advantages of superior leadership.

We may be forced to sign up yet.

9 Monumental Pets

There are some famous animals. There are some animals that are almost as famous as people. Further, there are some famous people who owe a certain portion of their fame to an association they have had with animals. You have already read about Jonah and his whale, or should we say the whale and its Jonah? We know Cleopatra achieved a certain fame because of an asp, though we do not wish to rob Antony of his due. So here is a very small sampling of some mythical and some real animals that are famous or have brought fame to their owners.

HANNIBAL

Hannibal managed to get a group of elephants across the Alps through Saint Bernard Pass into Italy. For this he was considered a military genius. Later on he was met in battle by Scipio Africanus whose brilliant strategy consisted of moving the troops out of the way of the elephants when they charged. For this reason *he* was considered a military genius. Actually one was a good road builder and the other a good traffic policeman.

ANDROCLES AND THE LION

Androcles nursed a lion in the jungle and befriended it. Much later on and many miles away Androcles was to meet this same lion in the arena. The lion didn't eat Androcles as he was supposed to. For this reason the critics in the morning papers gave the performance very poor reviews, though a few members of the audience secretly thought the ending just fine. Many Christians were eaten by lions in other tragic performances, and undoubtedly the critics raved. But history, the final moderator in such matters, liked the trick ending better.

ROBERT THE BRUCE

Robert the Bruce, loser of four battles and in hiding, watched a spider in a cave. Four times the spider tried to spin its web by anchoring to an attachment point. Four times the spider failed. But on the fifth try, the spider succeeded. Inspired by this picture of perseverance, Robert the Bruce assembled his armies once more, fought, and won. Lost to many, and perhaps someday to all, are the reasons for the battle. But it will be long remembered that Robert the Bruce was inspired by a spider. Some might think he was a fool for following such light inspiration and an even bigger fool for admitting it. But then, great wills need small inspirations to put them on their way. So here's to Robert and his spider too!

THE HORSE THAT WASN'T

The blank space above is dedicated to the horse that wasn't. This was the horse that Richard the Third was willing to trade a kingdom for. "My kingdom for a horse," he cried. But the horse never showed up, so we don't know whether Richard would really have made the trade, because he was not a very honest person, according to Shakespeare. Not only that, but if the horse had shown up, how could Richard have deeded a kingdom to it when the horse couldn't even have signed its own name? So horse-that-wasn't, it is just as well you didn't show up to find out whether Richard meant it or not, because if he did mean it, there would have been a horse, or perhaps a succession of horses, sitting on the throne of England. Though we do suspect that some of the kings of England, as well as those of other countries, could have used a little more "horse sense."

GROUND HOG

February 2 is Groundhog Day. It is on that day that this weather prophet is supposed to come out of its burrow and take a quick look around. If it sees its shadow it will run back into the burrow because winter will be a long, hard one. If it does not see its shadow it is supposed to stay out for a while, signifying that winter will soon be over. Groundhogs have been superseded largely by space capsules with ingenious cameras and marvelous electronic brains. However, we suspect the groundhog is still holding his own on a percentage basis. Certainly he is cheaper to run.

THE STORK

The stork, as every one knows, brings children into the world. This is a labor of love which causes storks to work excessive hours, with the unfortunate result that in the next two hundred years people will have to stand on each other's heads for lack of room. Many agencies have suggested methods of controlling the population explosion. Our plan is really quite simple: Unionize all storks. Put them on a twenty-four hour week with paid vacations. Who knows? It's quite possible that they might go on a sit-down or a perched-up strike. This would settle things, probably permanently.

THE REPUBLICAN ELEPHANT AND
DEMOCRATIC MULE

The symbol of the Democratic Party is the mule. Republicans have pointed out that not only are most Democrats as stubborn as mules, but also there is an unmistakable similarity between a mule and a jackass. Not to be outdone, the Democrats are pleased to point out that it takes, conservatively speaking, between eighteen and twenty-one months for a baby elephant to arrive in this world, and that it takes at least that many years for a Republican to have a new idea.

CHER AMI

Cher Ami was the most famous pigeon of World War I, perhaps of history. During the war, a battalion had been cut off. No one knew where it was, so it became the "Lost Battalion." The Lost Battalion sent pigeons out with word of its location, but the birds were all shot down. However, Cher Ami, with part of her leg shot off, managed to get through to headquarters. What drove Cher Ami on, no one will ever know. Perhaps she ate a better brand of birdseed. But she saved many lives. The only birdbrains in that entire operation belonged to those gentlemen who managed to misplace an entire battalion in the first place.

The first near-human in space was a monkey. Contrary to some of the experiences of human astronauts, the monkey was trained so well that not once during his entire flight did he push the wrong botton or leave a system on for too long a time. Furthermore, when the monkey was put back into the harness to indicate whether he wanted to go again or not, he was sensible enough to refuse. The astronautical monkey joins that gathering host of monkeys who have become famous. We already have the great monkey artist who paints so superbly in the modern style that he took first prize in an art show. Perhaps it is only a matter of time before some monkey wins the Nobel prize for writing a marvelous and comprehensive treatise on the irrational behavior of humans. Then we will no longer be friends with them.